DANCE SMART

CONCEPTS FOR ALL
HIP-HOP DANCE STYLES

FraGue Moser-Kindler

Cover and Illustrations by Philipp Lampert
Edited by Abigail Summers
Photo of the Author by Simon Kupferschmied

ISBN: 9781697871081
Independently published by FraGue Moser-Kindler
via Kindle Direct Publishing

Contents

Chapter 4
Working with the Music

Chapter 5
Creating New Material

Chapter 6
Practical Concepts Drawn from Urban Dance

About this book

Dancing is an activity that belongs to the artistic field, within which the learning process never ends throughout your whole life. This is due to the liveliness of dancing and its constant development. Not only does the discipline evolve constantly, but also the dancer.

The first steps into the dancing world often take place in a course that focuses mainly on choreography or technique. Sooner or later, the ambitious dancer will want to embark on a journey in order to make the dance his own. The concepts presented serve as an introduction to the world of independent development in your dancing.

They give guidance on HOW to individually evolve without expecting premature results.

The concepts presented help:
• To develop new movement material.
• To craft your own choreographies or create freestyles on the spot.
• To become mentally "free" while dancing.

When working with these concepts, a few basic rules should be carefully observed so as to get the most out of them:

1. Quantity over quality: As in a brainstorming session on any other topic, you should not make any assessment of the results at the beginning of the work.

2. It is about getting used to this work process at the beginning. The more conceptual dance work is practised, the faster and deeper you can comprehend the matter.

3. Playful approach: Each of these concepts should be approached in the most relaxed way possible. They all serve our growth. No matter whether we deal with it "correctly" or "wrongly," our dancing unfolds.

4. "Goofing around" within the concepts is fun, and helps to stay longer focused. Group work reinforces this effect.

The magic occurs when you deepen and lose yourself in the moment. Depth results through the frequent occupation with a theme. The better you know the material, the deeper you can dig. Immersing yourself in what you do results from "not thinking too much." When both things come together, it is only a matter of time until remarkable results are being achieved.

When we work on a performance, a show or a play, we should only work with the magic that arises in those special moments. After all, this kind of material is really individual and unique ... but it takes time.

I kept this book short. This is on purpose as I think we should spend our time exploring the concepts presented instead with reading about them. Concepts are not meant to be science but a source of inspiration for your dance. So don't worry if you execute any of the following ideas precisely as someone else or in your way. As long as your dance is growing, they do their duty. In today's non-fiction writing, it's state of the art to enrich the material with motivating stories. I tried to do that, but it did not feel right for this book. So I got rid of all the stories in the editing process. If you disagree with this decision after reading through the book, let me know. My email is at the end of the book.

Why this book?

During my years of teaching, I mainly taught movement material, freestyle and musicality in my classes. In recent years, I took a break from teaching due to other priorities, but I did a lot of substitutions for other dance teachers.

Since I only see these students occasionally and can't work with them on a regular schedule, I try to give them useful material, which they can use on their own. So, I teach concepts that help the students to further improve their understanding of "How to apply the dance stuff that I already know." During these lessons, the question often arose whether these concepts existed anywhere in writing. Since I could not name a source, I decided to write this book.

It is directed towards ambitious beginners and advanced dancers who want to broaden their dancing beyond fixed choreographies.

How to use it?

This book is meant to be a constant training companion and should germinate thought-provoking impulses when in search of new challenges.

I recommend that you first read through all the concepts, and then try them out during the training sessions according to your individual preferences and mood.

As soon as you are familiar with all the concepts, you can determine the daily dance challenge by chance. What you need is a regular six-sided dice. The first dice roll decides on the chapter of the book, the second decides on the concept itself.

To increase the difficulty, several concepts can be combined. It is an excellent idea to combine an idea from chapter 4 with another randomly selected concept. Thus, one is forced to pay attention to the music and the movement at the same time.

Terms and Definitions

A few words before we really get started.

When I talk about (movement) vocabulary in the book, I mean the amount of movements available to a dancer. If I have a larger vocabulary in a language, I can express myself more selectively. The same applies to dance. I use this term synonymously with material. I also use it to describe my vocabulary.

When we speak of levels, we mean different heights of movement. These are roughly divided in jumping, standing, squatting, sitting and lying.

When I write dynamics, I mean the differences in size, speed, force and the other parameters.

Chapter 1

The Basics

The concepts that are presented here are the essential tools with which we will encounter every movement and every sequence of movements.

They contain questions with which we juxtapose our existing as well as our new movement vocabulary. The subtleties inherent in every idea become visible through these elementary methods, and show us what can be done with a movement or sequence.

Some of these concepts have more complex relatives with which we will deal later.

These are the basics that over time will become second nature to us, so much that we will eventually apply them without thinking.

1.1 Direction/Rotation

THE CONCEPT OF DIRECTION SHOWS US MOVE-
MENTS FROM DIFFERENT DIRECTIONS AND LEADS
TO VARIATIONS OF THE SAME, CAUSED ONLY BY
CHANGING THE ORIENTATION IN THE SPACE.

Every step and every movement in our vocabulary can be po-
sitioned anywhere in space. In class, we usually work in rooms
with mirrors. This results in a fixed "front," which leads to a
fixed orientation in the room. Most movements are performed
with a focus on the mirror.

If we consciously choose our orientation in the room, different
images result for the viewer (or for ourselves when checking
ourselves in the mirror) without changing the step itself.

A variant thereof would be the "rotation," where we change the
orientation during the move.

For easy understanding, we will think in four different directions: Front, left, back and right. From each of these directions,
a movement appears optically different. To achieve further re-
finement, there are also the directions front left, front right,
rear left and rear right. These are the diagonals, which have a
precise angle between the four primary designations. As with a
compass, this subdivision can be refined at will.

As we begin to work with this concept, we look at our
movements from all directions. Once we are familiar with
it, we also change the direction during the movement.
Changing the direction during a move creates many exciting possibilities.

1.2 Size

THE SIZE CONCEPT TAKES THE MOVE THROUGH THE WHOLE RANGE OF POSSIBILITIES THAT RESULT FROM MAKING IT BIGGER OR SMALLER. THIS DOES NOT REALLY CREATE NEW VARIATIONS, BUT THE OPTICS AS WELL AS THE FEELING OF A MOVEMENT CHANGE SIGNIFICANTLY WITH THE SIZE.

Every movement can be changed in its size. For example, this happens by making larger or smaller steps. With stretched arms and legs, every move looks and feels different than with angled ones.

Even when stretching, you can try to stretch a few more centimeters than you are actually used to. On the other hand, the movement size can be greatly reduced by tightening the limbs.

The contrast created by small and large interpretations of the same movement or by different movements of different sizes leads to a great dynamic.

As an exercise, we take a well-known movement in the size that we have learned. Now, we try to extend the dimensions of all parts of the movement as far as possible. If we are satisfied with the result, the next step is to reduce the size of the movement.

As a further exercise, we improvise with different sized interpretations of the same movement to see how these changes affect us.

An additional option is to leave most of the movement as it is and apply the concept of magnification/minimization to just one detail. For example, feet are moving as usual, and only upper body or hand movement size is varied.

1.3 Energy

THE CONCEPT OF ENERGY BRINGS FORTH DIFFERENT INTENSITIES BY CHANGING THE QUALITY OF THE MOVEMENT.

The point here is that movements are performed with different amounts of energy. Depending on the dancer, energy is interpreted differently, and therefore it is rather a subjective matter. For many people the term is synonymous both with force/strength and body tension. However, this does not necessarily apply to everyone.

Unlike Size, Energy does not have to affect the magnitude of the movement. It can, but it is not a necessary criterion. Neither is it directly related to speed, although for many people an increase in energy is also associated with an increase in speed.

To me, the easiest way to explain energy is in connection with the state of "being well-rested."

If I want to snuggle in my blanket in the morning and don't want to get up at all, my energy level is low.

If I am pumped up with adrenaline in a competition while waiting for my turn, the energy level is high.

As an exercise, try yourself on a known movement - As if you don't feel like doing it at first, and then as if your life depends on it.

Afterwards you take the movement, start at one energetic extreme and gradually work your way back and forth to the other extreme.

1.4 Travelling

TRAVELLING SENDS OUR MOVEMENTS ON A VOYAGE OF DISCOVERY INTO SPACE, GIVING US THE OPPORTUNITY TO SHAPE IT AND FIND VARIATIONS THAT ARISE FROM NECESSARY CHANGES TO THE MOVEMENT MATERIAL.

With almost every movement, we can travel a path in space. This can happen spontaneously, or we fix a path before the execution, which must be followed.

Both path and direction open up a vast number of possibilities, since every path can be covered in every direction.

First of all, we simply try to travel with any movement that is normally stationary. Forwards, to the sides and backwards. Just like the "compass" we used for the Directions. Then, we try to cover these paths at different speeds and/or take more complicated paths.

For exercise purposes, we select a movement that is normally stationary and explore the entire available training or rehearsal space with it.

Selecting a standard movement path, and traveling a different path with this movement can also use this concept.

A roll normally travels along a linear path. In this case, we would try to force a curve. If a step normally goes to the side, we try to make it forward or backward.

1.5 Speed

THE CHANGE OF THE MOVEMENT'S EXECUTION SPEED DOES NOT CHANGE THE MOVEMENT IT- SELF, BUT LEADS TO DIFFERENT PERSPECTIVES OR FOCUSES ON NEW ASPECTS. JUST LIKE LANGUAGE, YOU CAN DIRECT THE ATTENTION OF THE AUDI- ENCE THROUGH YOUR OWN TEMPO.

Depending on the dance style in which our origins lie, we learn some movements at a certain tempo. However, the speed of each movement should also be seen as a variable.

Our range of speeds should be as wide as possible: From "as fast as possible" to "super slow motion."

The motion's aesthetics change significantly with speed.

An exercise of the concept: We choose any movement and repeat it a few times at normal speed. Next, we try to make the movement as fast as possible. Then, we slow down the movement and finally try to draw it over a really long peri- od of time. As if it were filmed with an ultra-slow motion camera.

It should be noted that the speed of a movement does not have to change the energy or effort used. Even a slow movement can be performed with a lot or little energy.

In addition, we can only subject certain parts of a movement to acceleration or deceleration and thus make further interest- ing modifications.

1.6 Levels

IF YOU MOVE AT DIFFERENT HEIGHTS, YOU GET
VARIATIONS OF THE SAME MATERIAL.

It is often worth trying a movement at several height levels.
This doesn't always work, but usually very interesting new possibilities emerge.

Possible levels are: Jumping (in the air), on the toes, standing,
squatting (different heights), sitting and/or lying.

At first glance, it seems to us that many movements cannot
simply be transported to other levels. With a little imagination,
however, this is practically always possible.

A standing movement can, in any case, be carried out in all
standing variations and "analogously" nearly always while sitting.

For practice, we take two movements. One of them
should contain footsteps, the other should not. Now, we
go through all possible levels with this movement. We
start with the original height, and then reduce the height
further and further. The different standing levels usually
don't cause any problems. In sitting and lying, you can actually perform the steps of one movement on the ground
or pretend to have your feet in the air.

To translate the movement into the jump can be a bit more
complicated depending on the duration of the movement, since
the time available before touching the ground again is limited.

DEVELOPMENT
OF
EXISTING MATERIAL

Chapter 2

Development of existing Material

The next chapter is dedicated to the exploration and further development of the material which we have already acquired. We focus on movements from our active movement vocabulary, and test how far we can go with them.

Since this chapter (as well as the previous one) is built on our existing material, it is very well suited as an introduction if you have not yet worked with concepts.

2.1 Expand

THROUGH EXPAND, YOU GET LONGER VARIA-
TIONS OF ALREADY EXISTING MOVES.

Expand means to add to or to prolong an existing movement.
This is done by simply attaching more material.

A simple way of expanding is to do a small part of the movement twice. For example, a kick and a step to the side becomes
a kick with two steps to the side. With this concept, you can
always develop your own sequences, for the new material can
also be edited with Expansion.

How and in what way you extend the movement is purely a
matter of interpretation and personal preference.

As an exercise, we choose a relatively short movement and
add another movement. You could take a lot of time to find
suitable movements (as you should in the process of creating a stage play), but in this case, we simply take the first
addition that comes to mind so as to increase the speed of
the process. In the beginning, quantity beats quality. If
you concentrate too much on finding the right movements,
you can easily come to a halt as you are not satisfied with
the result. The better results come with practice.

2.2 Cut

CUT CREATES CUT-OUTS FROM KNOWN MATERI-
AL. SUPERFLUOUS MATERIAL IS DELETED, AND
EMPHASIS IS PLACED ON A SPECIAL PART OF THE
MOVE.

Cut is the opposite of Expand. It reduces the size of a movement or omit parts.

This reduces complex movements or interesting details into
smaller units.

During practice, we take a complex movement with many
details and "cut" parts away. The resulting new movement
can be further reduced.

2.3 Mix

MIX CREATES NEW COMBINATIONS OF EXISTING MATERIAL.

By mixing, I take parts of one movement and combine them with parts of another movement. Thus, new combinations are created.

For example, I start with the kick of a classic "Kick Ball Change" and combine it with a "Pirouette."

This often results in exciting creations by combining styles or inserting movements within a style that do not normally occur together. Of course, there is no reason not to mix related or similar movements. There is no difference. Only the quality of the components is decisive. :-)

We start the exercise with three movements. We divide these into two halves and combine each beginning with each end. This helps to record which combinations we have already used.

Later, we take any part of movements and put them together as it pleases us. Here, too, "quantity over quality" applies at the beginning.

If you combine Expand, Cut and Mix, you enter a puzzle of movements.

2.4 Fill in the Blanks

IN THE CONCEPT OF FILL IN THE BLANKS, NEW DETAILS ARE ADDED TO EXISTING MOVEMENTS. THEREFORE, IT IS WELL SUITED TO EMBELLISH CHOREOGRAPHIES.

With this concept, you can tune multi-part movements. Let's take a step left, step right as an example. Between the two steps, there is room for an additional movement. The space in between is filled with a new movement.

Fill in the Blanks works both on the pure movement level and musically. If a rhythm offers room for an additional move-ment, I can fill it up. In this case, one would maintain the basic rhythm and fill the pauses with fast movements.

As an exercise, we choose a movement that consists of at least two distinct parts. In the middle of these two parts, we insert additional movements.

Depending on your own working pace, you can very quickly find movement variations, which can also be created on the fly during the dancing.

If you start with the musical aspect, search for the pauses or the slow movements in a sequence and replace them with faster movements.

2.5 Chinese Whispers

THE CHINESE WHISPERS ARE USED TO QUICK-
LY CREATE SUCCESSIVE VARIATIONS THAT MOVE
FURTHER AND FURTHER AWAY FROM THE SELECT-
ED SOURCE MATERIAL. SINCE THE INDIVIDUAL
VARIATIONS CAN ONLY CONTAIN SMALL CHANG-
ES, THE GENERAL STYLE OF THE MOVEMENTS USU-
ALLY REMAINS.

This concept is based on the children's game "Chinese Whispers." You can play the game in a group, much like the original,
or you can "play" alone. While the actual "whispers" try to pass
on the message as correctly as possible, in this case we change a
single detail or aspect of the movement.

We take this new movement as a starting point for the next
round. The more often we repeat this process, the more movement variations we get.

After numerous repetitions, the new movements are radically
different from the original material.

2.6 In and Out

IN AND OUT HELPS TO BREAK UP REPETITIVE PAT-
TERNS IN OUR DANCING OR HELPS TO DISGUISE
THEM.

Every dancer faces the reality that he prefers to execute certain move sequences or falls back into them in case of uncer-
tainty. The 'In and Out concept' is able to frame these movements and give the dancer more possibilities to get in and out
of them.

Choose a move and look for 10 (each number works, but the
higher the number, the better) movements, which can be performed immediately afterwards. Then, you look for 10 movements that can be executed before it. With these 20 moves, you
have 100 possibilities to present one original move.

FREESTYLE AND CHOREOGRAPHY DESIGN

Chapter 3

Freestyle and Choreography Design

Freestyle is a term that appears in many different contexts. Therefore, it often presents different meanings according to different dancers.

For the purpose of this chapter, freestyle is the creation of the dance while doing it.

The opposite is a previously fixed choreography. In this case, the dancer already knows the exact sequence beforehand.

I have learned most of the concepts presented in this book in conjunction with freestyle. But of course, they can also be used to create fixed choreographies. After all, freestyle is choreographing while dancing.

3.1 Equilibrium

EQUILIBRIUM TAKES THE FOCUS AWAY FROM THE
MOVEMENT WHEN DANCING OR CHOREOGRAPH-
ING AND DIRECTS IT ON BALANCING THE DIREC-
TIONS.

Equilibrium is a choreographic or freestyle composition concept. The choreography must be balanced in all directions.
There are many variations of Equilibrium with different names,
the only difference between them is how complex the align-
ments are, and how they have to be balanced.

- "Pendulum" is the simplest option and means: For every
  movement to the right, there must be a movement to the left.
- "Four Corners" on the other hand, requires to complete
  each corner of a square or rectangle before arriving at that
  corner again. The order of the corners does not matter.
- "Triangle" and "Octagon" work the same, but the shapes
  involved are triangles or octagons. The geometric shape
  you choose is not decisive.

The individual movements and their extent depend on the
dancer's interpretation. For some, a step to the left may only be
balanced by a step to the right, but for others a look in the other
direction may suffice.

This is not about mathematics, but about adhering to a struc-
tural criterion.

To start the exercise, we simply apply a "left-right balance."
For each movement that we make in one direction, a movement
in the other direction is followed, before we can return to the
original direction. Later, we add additional dimensions (front -
back, top - bottom).

3.2 Energy Ball

ENERGY BALL FOCUSES ON THE MANIPULATION OF AN IMAGINARY OBJECT. THUS, THE MOVEMENT CREATION BECOMES MORE PLAYFUL, INSTEAD OF BEING BASED SOLELY ON THE TECHNIQUE.

This approach requires a little more imagination than the previous concepts. For this concept, imagine that there is an energy ball in space that you manipulate with your own body. Depending on the interpretation, the energy ball has different characteristics:

- It floats in space and is passive. In this case, the ball is set in motion by the movements of the dancer's body.
- It has an increased attraction. The body of the dancer is attracted to the ball.
- It pushes the body of the dancer away from itself.
- The ball is sent out into space by the dancer's body and comes back.
- The energy moves only within the dancer's body.

No matter which option you choose, it is important to follow certain basic rules so that the concept works well.

1. You have to get involved with the play.
2. The focus of the body (gaze, alignment, attention) should follow the ball and its movements.

As an exercise, we imagine an energy ball which we have to send on a demanding journey across our rehearsal room through the movements of our body.

STORY TELLING

3.3 Storytelling

STORYTELLING IS A CONCEPT FOR CREATING CHO-REOGRAPHIES OR FREESTYLE DANCING THAT FO-CUSES ON TELLING A STORY.

It is a concept that's being implanted by drama. You take a theme and work on it in your dancing. The theme can be simple (for example a walk in the forest or intense heat) or tell a complex story. Different dancers work with different detailing degrees.

There are several approaches:

1. Translate the story into dancing. A potential spectator will be able to recognize the story. In this case, there is a chance of drifting into a dance-like acting. Depending on the intended use, this may or may not be desired.

2. The second approach would be the question: "How might the dance of someone that experienced the story look like?" All acting is banned. Only the mood of the story and the emotions are captured.

3. "Dialogue Method:" Multi-person use. A dialogue with words is developed at the beginning. Next, the words are accompanied by dancing movements. Afterwards, the words are omitted and the movements are refined and provided with facial expressions, energy, and emotion.

The dialogue method can be observed in my short movie 'Elsewhere'. You can find it on my website www.frague.at or on youtube and vimeo.

As an exercise, we choose a theme and work on it with all three approaches.

→] CONST
RAINTS

3.4 Constraints

CREATIVE RESTRICTIONS LEAD YOU TO DEAL WITH MOTIONS AND OBSTACLES THAT WOULD NORMALLY BE AVOIDED. THIS CREATES NEW MOVEMENT MATERIAL.

It's a familiar concept among all creative professions. You impose restrictions on yourself that force you to break new ground.

In the simplest instance, you are not allowed to use your "favorite movements." This alone forces you to improvise.

Basically, the possibilities of limitations are restricted only by your own imagination. A (certainly not complete) list of possibilities:

- Certain body parts may not be used.
- Only certain body parts may be used.
- Only movements/no standing motions.
- Only jumps/no jumps.
- Only squat movements/no squat movements.
- Only ground movements/no ground movements.
- The hands must not touch the ground.
- The feet must not touch the ground.
- Hands and feet must always touch the ground.
- The hands (or just one hand) must always touch a specific body part (For example the head).
- Certain paths in the room are forbidden (see Ways and Time) or mandatory.
- The sequence must always turn in the same direction or must never follow it.

3.5 Ways and Time

THE CONCEPT OF 'WAYS AND TIME' HELPS TO IM-
PROVISE MOVEMENTS BY PLACING THE MENTAL
FOCUS ON THE PATHS TO BE COVERED.

This concept should not be confused with the Travelling concept presented at the beginning of the book. At the beginning
of the book, it is about the idea that it is possible to travel a path
with any step.

In Ways and Time, a path is fixed and the time period in which
this path is covered is defined.

You can define whether the path is a one-way street or whether
you can move in both directions.

One exercise, for example, defines a straight line that has
to be traversed very slowly, or a winding path that has to
be mastered at a high speed. Both are one-way paths with
the possibility to move in both directions.

In order to break out of the own patterns, it is advisable to in-
volve a second person for the definition of the task.

Ways and Time also works if you only choose a path without a
time limit. In this case, however, it is actually only a matter of
Ways.

3.6 Focus Concepts

FOCUS CONCEPTS ARE HELPFUL WHEN IMPROVIS-
ING OR DEVELOPING CHOREOGRAPHIES, TOO, AS
THE MENTAL FOCUS IS PLACED ON ORIENTATIONS
IN SPACE.

Rather than a single concept, it is a collection of ideas that all
have one common denominator: The dancer's focus.

The focus of the dancer is to concentrate on a single point. This
point can as well change during the dance, but doesn't have to
do so.

The focus point can be in the audience, somewhere on the
stage, somewhere outside the stage; it can be on another dancer
or on one of the dancer's body parts.

Conventional focus points:
- The audience.
- A certain person in the audience.
- Technique.
- The stage sides.
- Backstage.
- The stage center.
- The floor.
- A particular point of the stage set or any object in the
  training room.
- Another dancer.
- The own hand (it can be any part of the body, but the hand
  is a stable).

Every conceivable point is equally possible.

Variants would be:
- Always or never look where the movement goes.
- The gaze initiates a movement or follows a movement.

WORKING WITH THE MUSIC

Chapter 4

Working with the Music

The following concepts deal with different ways of dealing with music. Some of them are simply rules regarding which parts of the music to use, others work with complex procedures that can help to develop new movements.

DOMINANT SOUND

4.1 Dominant Sound

DOMINANT SOUND SHOWS WHAT PARTS OF THE MUSIC ARE PERCEIVED AS DOMINANT.

The movement follows the dominant instrument/sound in the music. The dominant sound is the one that comes to the fore the most.

This perception is of course very subjective. Different people can respond to different frequencies, therefore, for one dancer the bass can be the dominant sound, while someone else perceives the voice as the dominant sound.

To practice, we play several songs from any playlist and adjust our movements to the dominant sound. This sound is different in each track, and can also be different for each listener.

4.2 My House

WITH THE MY HOUSE CONCEPT, WE SUCCESSIVE-LY SHOW ALL MUSICAL PARTS IN OUR ORDER OF CHOICE.

My house is a guided tour through our own house. At home, every nook and cranny is known and each room is shown to the visitor one after the other, not all at the same time.

Likewise, all musical instruments are presented in the same way, according to what is most appealing to you. For example, you can dance first to the beat, then to the guitar, piano, voice, returning to the drums...

As an exercise, we take one track from our existing music collection and a second one we don't know. We listen to the first song carefully beforehand, and try to listen to all the instruments. Then, dance to the different instruments in any order. With the second track, we start the music and dance straight away without listening to it first. This way the sound is discovered while dancing.

POLY RHYTHM METER

4.3 Polyrhythm & Polymeter

POLYRHYTHM AND POLYMETER ARE MATHEMAT-ICAL-MUSICAL CONCEPTS, BY WHICH COMPLEX MOVEMENTS ARE CREATED, WHICH DEMAND OUR COORDINATION.

Polyrhythm is when different rhythms are overlaid, thereby creating a new rhythm.

An example: If a four-to-the-floor beat and a triplet rhythm are combined, they only meet at the full counts of the bar. All other beats of the two rhythms do not meet.

This creates very complex movement patterns. In practice, one would dance a movement with one part of the body in one rhythm and with another part in the other.

A polymeter, on the other hand, is when different time-signatures come together. Thus, the two movements do not meet at the beginning of each bar but only after several bars, whose duration depends on the chosen time signatures.

A simple example: The feet make normal steps, counted 1, 2. Then, the pattern repeats itself. The hands draw a triangle in the air, counted 1, 2, 3. Then repeating. The entire pattern is repeated only starting from bar unit 3 of the second bar (counted in 4/4 times).

In this example, even counting beats are used. This means an even tempo in all movements.

The length of the movements is chosen according to personal taste when practicing or by the music when freestyling.

If this exercise becomes too easy, the counting beats can be varied so that both movements do not progress at the same speed. For example, the arms can make two movements while the legs do four, odd and even counts can converge. The whole thing becomes particularly demanding when one part is performed on an even rhythm (e.g. 4 movements) and the other part on an odd rhythm (e.g. 3 movements), but both at different speeds.

Any rhythms can be overlaid on top of each other.

With increasing difficulty, this exercise resembles more of a mental exercise or a drummer's practice.

The introductory exercise: The feet make normal steps, the hands make a pattern of four movements first, and then three. We then double the speed for feet or hands.

MUSICAL LAYERING

4.4 Musical Layering

WITH THE CONCEPT OF MUSICAL LAYERING, SEV-
ERAL MUSICAL ELEMENTS ARE DEPICTED SIMUL-
TANEOUSLY WHEN DANCING. THIS RESULTS IN A
VERY DETAILED VISUALIZATION.

Basically, this is a variant of polyrhythm, but it differs in its execution, since the planning of the rhythms is replaced by precise listening.

In this case, dancing is done with one body part following one instrument, and with the other body parts, any number of other instruments.

A standard example:

The feet dance to the basic beat of the drums, while the arms and the upper body to the leading melody. Head and shoulders are used for emphasis or other instruments.

The concept is similar to My House. The difference is that several room/music components are shown at the same time.

We start with a body part of our choice and assign it to the simplest part of the music piece - if possible a repetitive part, which we can repeat as soon as we understand it. Then, we choose another musical part and dance to it without stop executing the first part. We continue for as long as we can.

MISSING

4.5 Missing Instrument

WITH THE CONCEPT OF MISSING INSTRUMENT, THE DANCER TRIES TO WRITE AN ADDITIONAL VOICE TO THE MUSIC.

This is one of the most widespread and at the same time the most misunderstood musical concepts. Most people practice Missing Instrument without ever having heard of it. The idea is "To do something that goes well with the music." That is, the tempo fits and the basic rhythm is kept, otherwise, it's just about right. It's like playing an instrument that doesn't exist in the music. It's a suitable improvisation, similar to jazz music.

But in order to play an instrument that goes well with it, a little musical knowledge is highly needed; what would fit well and what would not, must be well known. It's not for nothing that jazz is considered a very demanding musical genre.

Missing Instrument is a legitimate concept for musical interpretation. But all those who try it should really pay attention to playing a nice additional instrument instead of falling into the celebration of repetitive rhythmic patterns.

At the beginning, we take existing musical material and create smaller variations of it. That way we are still very close to the source material, but without doing the same thing.

Gradually, we move away from the existing material, but try to keep a close connection with the instruments and the music groove.

SOUNDTRACK METHOD

4.6 Soundtrack Method

THE INSPIRATION FOR THE MOVEMENT COMES FROM THE MUSIC'S EMOTIONAL CONTENT.

The connection between music and movement depends exclusively on mood and emotion. The music is allowed to have an effect on the listener, and it is then interpreted as dance.

Hollywood sends its greetings. Music is used in many films to accompany the events in order to increase the emotional effect. This also works in dancing. The mood of the music is used and the movements are adapted to it.

This concept also carries the risk of slipping into dancing drama. As usual, this can be desired or not.

IGNORING THE MUSIC

4.7 Bonus: Ignoring the Music

A CONCEPT ACCORDING TO THE PRINCIPLE: IF YOU DON'T WANT TO BE DEPENDENT ON MUSIC.

Sounds vicious, but it's not.

Depending on your artistic point of view, there doesn't have to be a direct connection between dance and music.

Ignoring or counterpointing the music is also okay.

The exercise is very simple. There is no influence from the playing music. This is challenging in different ways depending on the dancer's background.

CREATING NEW MATERIAL

Chapter 5

Creating New Material

When new movement material is created, it is often advantageous to use different approaches to the already known methods. Of course, something new can also be created from existing material, but there is always the danger of falling back into familiar patterns.

The ideas that are presented here are intended to help you get out of the familiar patterns of the already automated material in order to find completely new movements.

STEAL
LIKE A
DANCER

5.1 Steal like a dancer

STEALING FROM AS MANY SOURCES AS POSSIBLE.

Taking inspiration from somewhere else is common in every art form. Regarding dancing, however, we don't mean the stealing of other dancers or choreographers, but the stealing of non-dancing material.

Movements from everyday life, sports, martial arts, sign language and every other area of life can serve as dancing models.

The movement is taken and changed at will until it is "enough dance" for our personal taste.

Within this process, we can of course use all the tools that we have come to know or will come to know in the future.

FALLING

5.2 Falling

THE BALANCE GAME SERVES AS A SOURCE FOR NEW MOVES.

Especially in contemporary dance, a popular concept is to play with balance and to let the body fall. To really fall down is actually only the extreme form of this idea.

The central focus is playing with gravity. Deliberately unbalancing your body in order to either catch it and bring it back into balance, or moving from one "falling" movement to the next.

Entry exercise: You stand upright and let your weight tilt easily in one direction. Only when you threaten to fall down, will you take a step to catch your body. If you are now balanced, you tend to repeat the principle. If you are not balanced, the process begins again of its own accord.

You can work with feet and hands if you have more control over your body. The weight is shifted alternately to hands and feet. The transition here is always a "falling."

A variation would be letting the body fall completely and using a "getting up" or "rising up" motion as a second movement.

FORM OF SHAPES

5.3 Forms as Shapes

WE DEVELOP NEW MOVEMENTS BY RECON-STRUCTING GEOMETRIC SHAPES WITH THE BODY.

In this case, any geometric shapes are built with the body. Rectangles, triangles and circles are the most popular forms, but also here it is wise to use your own imagination and discover new forms.

First you try to reproduce the chosen shape with your hands. As soon as this works well, you explore more and more possibilities. Legs, the upper body and head all follow the motion. In this exercise, you can work without music at the beginning, if this is helpful.

Another exercise: You form the selected shape with your hands. Bring it into a new position and change it by adding or removing body parts. The transitions from one form to the next can be precise, whereby the form is maintained, or the form can disappear during the transitions and then emerge again.

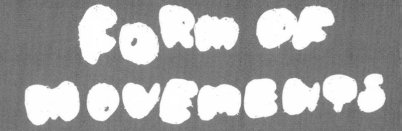

5.4 Forms as Movement

NEW MOVEMENTS FOLLOWING GEOMETRIC PAT-
TERNS.

This concept, like the previous one, is based on geometric shapes. However, the forms refer to movements in space instead of the actual images.

For example, only circular or linear movements are allowed. Whether they are executed with the entire body or with individual limbs, is of no importance.

As an exercise the arms are swung on paths that correspond to the chosen form. The same works with the feet and any other body part. Size, speed and intensity of the movements are freely selectable.

LEADING WITH

BODYPARTS

5.5 Leading with Bodyparts

WE DEVELOP STYLISTICALLY RELATED MOVE-
MENTS THROUGH UNIFORM MOTION IMPULSES.

With this concept, it is agreed that every movement must
have its starting point with a certain body part.

For example, each movement must begin with the left hand.
It is not important where the movement develops afterwards.
Only the beginning impulse is decisive.

As an alternative, the concept can also be used "upside down".
In this case, every movement would have to end in the corre-
sponding part of the body.

The starting or end point of the movement can remain fixed
or change during execution.

In an exercise session, the intention is to use every conceivable body part as a movement initiator. We start with the
hands, feet, knees, hips, stomach, chest, shoulders, elbows,
head, and whatever else comes to mind will as well follow.
The length of the movements is not relevant. However, the
initiating impulse must come from the leading part of the
body.

RANDOM ISATION

5.6 Randomisation

SOMETIMES IT'S BEST TO LET OTHERS DECIDE.

Choreographer Merce Cunningham and composer John Cage brought the 'chance element' into music and dance creation in modern dance times. Structures were previously created within which chance made the decisions. We can still use these resources today. For example, by making a list of instructions that are numbered, we allow the dice to decide on how to move. The instructions can be very concrete (move the left hand upwards in a circular motion) or very flexible (move downwards). The real work with this method lies in defining the parameters within which chance can reign.

As an exercise: Create a list with six very concrete and six very flexible instructions. Let the dice determine a sequence of ten instructions for both lists. We create a sequence of movements out of these combinations.

PRACTICAL CONCEPTS DRAWN FROM URBAN DANCE

Chapter 6

Practical Concepts Drawn from Urban Dance

The following chapter contains concepts that I have perceived as particularly inspiring in my own dance career, and as very powerful in the creative process.

They are based on urban dance technique (the hip-hop dance styles and funk styles). But I don't want to fail to mention that they also exist in other dance styles.

THREADING

6.1 Threading

CREATE OPTICALLY COMPLEX MOVEMENTS THROUGH A "TUNNEL EFFECT."

This is a concept that I personally only have experienced through urban dancing. You form a tunnel or a gate with your own body through which you pass with another part of your body.

Classic Threads are, for example, to put your hand to your shoulder, and go through with your head or hand, or with your hand to your foot, and go through with your other leg.

In the exercise, you try to find as many variations as possible on how to form tunnels with your own body. In the ideal case, the passage of one body part through the first tunnel already leads to the formation of another.

Threading also works very well as a concept with one or more partners.

6.2 Outlining

WITH THIS CONCEPT, WE CREATE MOVEMENT
SEQUENCES BY IMAGINARY "TRACING" OUR OWN
BODY.

Using outlining, the movements follow the outline of the
own body. Simply put, the outline is a reproduction of the body
shape. This can be done with the hands as well as with any other body part.

It is not important if there is a direct contact with the body's
outline or if it is pretended.

For practice, we try to find all outlining possibilities. Begin
by drawing the forms of your own body with your hands.
As soon as this is done, you try it with your feet. Then with
the head etc.

It is about finding out many different possibilities, and not
what works best. A multitude of possibilities leads to several
possibilities that work well.

TRACING

6.3 Tracing

WITH THIS CONCEPT, WE CREATE MOVEMENT SEQUENCES BY FOLLOWING ONE LEADING MOVEMENT OF THE BODY WITH THE OTHER MOVEMENTS.

Tracing is based on a similar idea to outlining. Here, however, no body shape is pursued, but a movement. One body part follows the movement of another body part.

The most common form of tracing is to support a wave; such as it occurs in popping.

Here, too, direct contact with the movement can exist, but it is not a must.

Just as with outlining, we try to explore all the possibilities that we have during practice. We follow movements with our hands first, and then with all other means that we can think of.

ACTION
REACTION

6.4 Action – Reaction

THIS CONCEPT LEADS TO A SERIES OF MOVEMENTS. EACH MOVEMENT MAY ONLY BEGIN AFTER THE PREVIOUS ONE HAS BEEN COMPLETED.

Action - Reaction describes a simple pattern in which each movement triggers a subsequent movement. So, the movements are never executed simultaneously, but strictly one after the other.

Each action triggers a reaction. In the simplest case, one movement directly triggers another by touching the next body part. However, there is no reason why one movement should not trigger a reaction in a completely independent part of the body.

As an introduction, we practice the following: Each movement must end at a different part of the body, which then conducts the next movement. Subsequently, the end of one movement triggers the next, no matter where on the body this happens.

Action - Reaction also works very well as a duet or in larger groups. The concept is then capable to create whole choreographies in an instant composition process.

CON NEC TIONS

6.5 Connections

THIS CONCEPT LEADS TO A PARALLEL SEQUENCE OF MOVEMENTS. SINCE EACH MOVEMENT, WHICH IS PART OF THE CONNECTION, IS ACCOMPANIED BY A FURTHER MOVEMENT.

In this process, one part of the body establishes an actual or imaginary connection with another. Through this connection, the connected body part can either guide the other movement or be guided by it.

For practice, we choose a movement that happens relatively isolated somewhere on the body. We place one hand on this isolated area and leave it there during the movement. Then, we try the same movement, but controlled by the hand.

We repeat this exercise, whereby the hand does not really touch the body part performing the isolated movement, but only follows it (imaginary connection).

Now, we can use less isolated movements or follow or lead with other parts of the body.

6.6 Fixpoint

FIXPOINT CREATES THE ILLUSION OF IMAGINARY SPACES THROUGH THE FIXATION OF INDIVIDUAL MOVEMENTS.

The concept has its origins in pantomime. It found its way to the urban dancers via popping. The Fixpoint fixes a body part at an imaginary point in space and meaning we can't move it away from there.

This forces us to find new ways in our dance to avoid breaking the illusion.

If we want to be very strict, Fixpoint is a very specific form of the Constraints approach.

Closing Remarks

The concepts and ideas presented above provide an introduction to the conceptual work that's associated with dancing. Every day, dancers around the world develop new ideas on how to deal with their expertise. Soon you will create your own concepts as well.

What matters is not the number of concepts we know, but a basic understanding of how we can make use of them. Once this has become part of our flesh and blood, it becomes very easy to work with a new concept.

Once you've worked through and understood this book, you won't have any problems with freestyles or inventing new moves. Enjoy the journey and stay open to new influences. Whether these influences originate from new teachers, new music or things that have nothing to do with dancing. Inspiration waits everywhere, you just have to be ready to see it.

About the Author

Franz Günter Moser-Kindler, aka FraGue, was not born as a dancer nor an artist. He spent his youth with martial arts and wears a black belt in Judo. He graduated as a software engineer and was deep into databases and web-development, when the insight struck that source code will not be the content of his life's work.

He made his hobby breaking (which is better known under the wrong term breakdance) the priority and didn't look back ever since. He performed in successful international shows with the dance companies Nobulus and Hungry Sharks. At the same time, he produced multiple dance theatre pieces and short movies with his own company Artfeeders. Now he is out to publish a series of practical guides for dance, dance-related productions, and dance business. Through the analytical thought process that he developed in his first job, he excels at understanding and explaining correlations and connections.

Discover more about FraGue on his blog www.frague.at.

May I Ask You A Favor?

Dance Smart is my first publication outside of the blogosphere, and I am working on building my name as a dance author.

For every author, but especially for new ones, it is essential to have reviews on their publications. These are used by the search engines to estimate the relevance of a book for potential readers. If you made it this far, please leave an honest review about Dance Smart at http://reviewdancesmart.frague.at.

It would also mean a lot to me when you recommend the book to a friend of yours, who is into dance as well.

If you have feedback, comments or questions, I look forward to your email at info@frague.at.

Thank you very much for reading my book. I honestly appreciate every one of you who took the time to dive into it. I hope it gives as much inspiration to you, as learning and discovering the concepts did to me.

Stay in Touch

Discovering the dance and art world is more pleasant with friends. When you like my writing, consider joining my Readers Group. It is an email list where I share weekly thoughts of inspiration, ideas that did not yet make it into the blog or a book or ask for your input on topics I work on.

Join my Readers Group at http://readersgroup.frague.at.

Made in the USA
Monee, IL
20 October 2021